MUSICAL
INSTRUMENTS
OF THE WORLD

Keyboards

M. J. Knight

W
FRANKLIN WATTS

An Appleseed Editions book

Paperback edition 2006

Franklin Watts
338 Euston Road
London NW1 3BH

Franklin Watts Australia
Hachette Children's Books
Level 17/207 Kent Street
Sydney NSW 2000

ISBN-10: 0 7496 6983 7
ISBN-13: 978 0 7496 6983 6

Dewey Classification: 786

Designed by Helen James
Created by Appleseed Editions Ltd, Well House,
Friars Hill, Guestling, East Sussex TN35 4ET

A CIP catalogue for this book is available from the British Library.

Photographs by Edwin Beunk, Corbis (Nubar Alexanian, Bettmann,
Burstein Collection, Christie's Images, DELLA ZUANA PASCAL/CORBIS SYGMA,
Henry Diltz, DUGOWSON/STM CONCEPT/CORBIS SYGMA, RUSSEIL
CHRISTOPHE/CORBIS SYGMA, Marc Garanger, Francoise Gervais, Philip Gould,
Hulton-Deutsch Collection, Bob Krist, Charles & Jesette Lenars, Roy McMahon,
Francis G. Mayer, Gianni Dagli Orti, Jose F. Poblete), The Lebrecht Collection

Printed in Thailand

Contents

Introducing keyboards

keyboards keyboards keyboards

This book is about instruments with keyboards. Keyboard instruments all sound when their keys are pressed. The sounds are made in various different ways.

Some of the oldest keyboard instruments, such as the harpsichord, sound when quills pluck the strings inside. The piano also has strings inside, but they are struck by small, felt-covered hammers to sound the notes.

A church organ has pipes which sound notes when air is pushed through them. An electronic organ creates notes from electric signals when its keys are pressed.

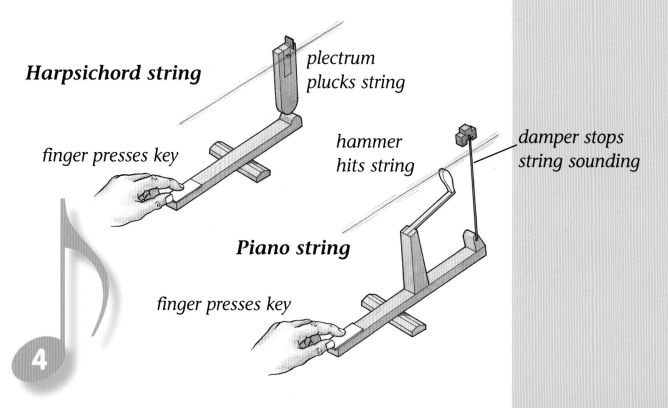

Harpsichord string

plectrum plucks string

finger presses key

hammer hits string

damper stops string sounding

Piano string

finger presses key

You can hear keyboard instruments playing all sorts of music in all sorts of places. Pianists perform classical music in concerts, and also accompany singers and other solo instruments. Jazz and dance music often have parts for a piano too.

The accordion and hurdy gurdy are traditional folk instruments. Their sound is loud and carrying, so they are often played in the open air at festivals and fairs.

Electronic organs and keyboards play a part in many pop and rock bands today. You can hear them on the radio, on CD, or live in concert.

A pianist accompanies a singer at a classical music festival in France. The piano lid is propped open for the performance.

Clavichord

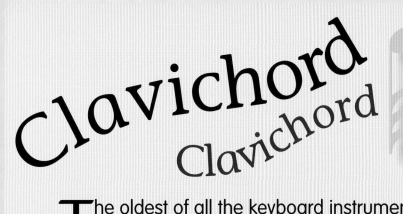

Clavichord Clavichord Clavichord Clavichord

The oldest of all the keyboard instruments is the clavichord. It looks like an oblong wooden box with an opening lid. Inside the box, pairs of metal strings are stretched lengthways, from end to end.

The keyboard of a clavichord is set towards the left hand side. When you press a key, a small metal blade called a tangent hits a pair of strings and sounds a note.

The clavichord has a very quiet voice and its sound is soft and gentle. Five hundred years ago it was the first keyboard instrument that people learned to play at home.

Arnold Dolmetsch made clavichords and harpsichords during the last century. His wife is helping him carry a clavichord.

L ike the clavichord, the virginal is an old instrument, which was first played nearly 500 years ago. It is shaped like a box and is often played on a table.

The keyboard of the virginal is small, and it can be in different positions, at either end or in the middle of the casing. When you press a key, a small quill (the hard middle part of a feather) plucks a string to sound a gentle, tinkling note.

Many virginals are beautifully decorated, with paintings of flowers or country landscapes on the lid and wooden casing.

This picture was painted 200 years ago and shows a woman sitting in front of her virginal. Can you see the picture painted inside the lid?

Harpsichord Harpsichord

Have you ever heard a harpsichord? It has a clear, crisp tone and can make a powerful sound. This beautiful old instrument looks a bit like a slender grand piano. Its outer casing is triangular-shaped and stands on four slim legs.

Harpsichords may have more than one keyboard. When you press a key, a small quill (the hard middle part of a feather) called a plectrum plucks the strings inside to make a note. There are two or more strings for each key.

This old French picture shows a woman accompanying two string players on the harpsichord in a very grand room.

Harpsichord

Did you know?

The quills inside a harpsichord were made from the wing and tail feathers of various birds, including crows, ravens, turkeys and eagles. Today they are usually made of plastic.

A harpsichord maker fits a key into place in a harpsichord with two keyboards.

A harpsichord player can choose how many strings to play by pulling out a small lever called a stop. If the player uses all the strings, the music is loud. Fewer strings make softer music.

Today you only hear the harpsichord occasionally, but 500 years ago many people played it. It also played an important part in orchestras during the 1700s.

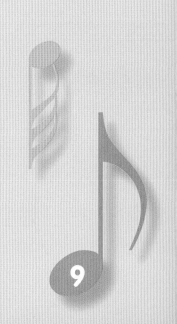

Spinet Spinet Spinet Spinet

The little sister of the harpsichord is the spinet. Three hundred years ago people played the spinet at home, partly because it was small and fitted easily into their homes.

Most spinets are triangular-shaped, with the keyboard on the shortest side of the triangle. When you press a key, a tiny quill (the hard middle part of a feather) plucks a string inside to sound the note. The sound is quiet and tinkling.

The wooden lid is propped up while the spinet is played, to make the sound louder.

This painting is called Musical Party. *Two men listen admiringly as a woman plays the spinet.*

Fortepiano

Fortepiano

Fortepiano is the name of an early version of the piano we know today. It was invented about 300 years ago by an Italian called Bartolomeo Cristofori, who built harpsichords.

His new instrument looked very like the harpsichord. The main difference is in the way the sound is made. When you press the keys of the fortepiano, the strings are hit by small hammers, instead of being plucked by quills. This makes a very different sound and means that the fortepiano can be played much louder than the harpsichord.

Can you see the difference between the keys on this fortepiano and the ones on the piano on page 14?

Fortepiano

Grand piano

True to its name, this piano is very grand! The largest grand pianos are nearly 3 metres long. They are called concert grands. Smaller grand pianos are called baby grands.

Grand pianos are made of wood, and have a strong iron frame inside to hold the strings. During a concert, the lid over the strings is propped open to make the sound louder.

When a pianist presses a key, a small hammer strikes a string inside to sound a note.

This pianist is playing a concert grand piano at the Evian Music Festival in France.

12

Inside a piano. One of the felt-tipped hammers at the bottom is hitting a string because the pianist has pressed a key.

Piano strings are different thicknesses: thick strings on the left side play low notes and thinner ones on the right side play higher ones. When the pianist lifts his finger off the key, a small pad called a damper falls against the string to stop it sounding (see page 4).

The grand piano has pedals which the pianist presses with his feet to change the sound of the notes. The right pedal keeps all the dampers away from the strings, and is called the sustaining pedal. Pressing this makes the sound of the piano fuller and richer. The left pedal makes the notes softer and quieter.

Did you know?

The winged shape of a grand piano is designed around the strings. The long bass (low) strings are on the left, and the shorter treble (high) strings on the right.

Upright piano
Upright piano

Many people learn to play the piano on an upright piano. This piano is named for its shape. It sits against a wall, and takes up much less space than its bigger cousin, the grand piano.

When you press a key on the piano, a small hammer hits a string inside to sound a note. The piano has two pedals, which you press with your feet: one makes the note longer and richer, while the other makes it softer.

Did you know?

Inside the piano the strings are stretched very tightly over an iron frame. It is strong enough to take a strain of 17 tons! Behind it is a soundboard, which makes the vibrations of the strings louder.

This boy is practising on his upright piano at home.

Melodica  Melodica

The melodica is a sort of mouth organ and makes the same kind of sound. You play it through a mouthpiece at one end.

The piano melodica has a set of keys along its length. You push these down to play a tune with the fingers of one hand, at the same time as blowing into the mouthpiece.

Inside the melodica are thin pieces of metal called reeds. When the air you blow into the mouthpiece moves across the reeds, they vibrate to make notes.

This unusual melodica is played by Buckwheat Zydeco at a concert in Louisiana, USA.

Melodica Melodica

Accordion Accordion Accordion

The accordion is a complicated instrument to play. You have to be strong to squeeze the pleated folds in the middle (called bellows) in and out. The squeezing pushes air over a set of thin pieces of metal called reeds, which make the notes.

While squeezing, the accordionist also plays a tune with his right hand on a keyboard on one side of the bellows. Each key plays two different notes – one when the bellows are squeezed together and a different one when they are pulled apart.

Clifton Chenier was a famous accordion player who was known as the King of Zydeco. Here he is playing at the New Orleons Jazz Festival.

16

The accordionist uses his left hand to press the finger buttons on the other side of the bellows. These sound chords as an accompaniment to the tune.

The accordion was invented nearly 200 years ago in Germany. Today you can hear it playing folk music in Europe and North and South America. It is an important instrument in cajun and zydeco music, which both grew up from the traditional folk music of Louisiana, in the USA.

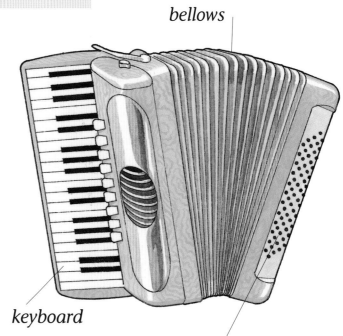

bellows

keyboard

finger buttons

Accordion Accordion Accordion

Did you know?

An old name for the accordion is the squeeze-box, because you have to squeeze it to play it.

Dulcitone

Dulcitone Dulcitone
Dulcitone Dulcitone

The sound of the dulcitone is soft and bell-like, like its name. This small wooden instrument stands on four slim legs.

Inside the dulcitone is a row of U-shaped metal bars of different sizes. When you press a key, a small hammer hits one of the bars to sound a note.

Inside the wooden case are the metal bars which sound the notes.

The dulcitone was invented in the 1800s by a Frenchman called Auguste Mustel, who lived in Paris. Its first name was the tuning fork piano.

Celeste Celeste Celeste

The celeste looks a bit like an upright piano, but it makes a different, bell-like sound when played.

Inside the wooden case are a row of steel bars. When you press a key, a tiny, felt-covered hammer hits one of the bars. Underneath each bar is a small hollow box which makes the sound louder.

You can hear the celeste in the ballet *The Nutcracker*, written by a Russian composer called Tchaikovsky. Listen for it in 'The Dance of the Sugar Plum Fairy'.

The celeste has one foot pedal which you press to make the sound louder. It is called the sustaining pedal.

Organn Organ Organ

The organ is one of the oldest and loudest musical instruments in the world. It has a row of pipes which sound notes when air is pushed through them. The smallest organ pipes are just a few centimetres long, while the longest are giants more than 19 metres long.

There are two types of organ pipe, which make different sounds. Flue pipes are open pipes with a mouthpiece. They can be open at one end or closed (stopped). A stopped pipe sounds a lower note than

This beautiful organ is in St Stephen's Cathedral in Passau, Germany. It has 17,000 pipes and is one of the largest organs in the world.

an open pipe. The other pipes are reed pipes, with thin metal reeds inside, which sound when air passes over them.

Organs have one or more keyboards, which are called manuals. Each keyboard is linked to rows of pipes which have levers called stops. The stops have names (such as flute or trumpet), which describe the sound they make when the organist pulls them out.

The biggest organs played today are in churches and cathedrals.

Did you know?

Many years ago the air which makes the organ play had to be pumped into the organ by hand through a set of bellows. Today it is pumped by an electric motor.

An organist plays on two different keyboards, or manuals, at the same time.

Harmonium

Harmonium

Harmonium

Harmonium

A harmonium sounds a bit like an organ. Its other name is the reed organ, because the sound it makes comes from a series of thin strips of metal called reeds.

When air is pushed over the reeds, they sound, making notes. The air is pumped into the instrument by a set of bellows which the harmonium player pushes with his feet.

The harmonium was invented about 200 years ago in France. It was often played in churches which didn't have an organ, or in people's homes.

A Russian monk plays the harmonium in a monastery near Tblisi in Georgia.

Ondes martenot

The ondes martenot is an electronic instrument invented in the 1920s by a Frenchman called Maurice Martenot.

Its keyboard is connected to speakers. When you press a key, a note is created electronically, then amplified (made louder) through the speakers. The sound is a strange, eerie wailing, half way between a hum and a voice singing 'oo'.

The instrument has controls to make the notes louder, softer or different in other ways. You can hear the ondes martenot in film soundtracks.

Did you know?

The word ondes is French for waves. The inventor used it to describe the smooth falling and rising sound of his instrument.

Maurice Martenot, who invented the ondes martenot. His sister, Ginette, is playing it.

Ondes martenot Ondes martenot Ondes martenot Ondes martenot Ondes marter

Hurdy gurdy

This ancient instrument looks like a thick and chunky violin, with a handle at one end. When you turn the handle, it turns a wheel underneath the strings and makes them vibrate.

On the side of the hurdy gurdy is a small keyboard. Pushing down the keys moves small wooden blades. These press against the strings to make different notes.

A musician wearing traditional costume plays the hurdy gurdy at a street festival in France.

Hurdy gurdy

Hurdy gurdy

This old painting shows that the hurdy gurdy has not changed much over the years.

The hurdy gurdy usually has four to six strings. Two of them play a single long note called a drone. The other strings play the tune.

Players hang the hurdy gurdy around their neck from a strap, or sit down to play with the instrument on their lap.

The first hurdy gurdys were played in medieval times. Travelling musicians called minstrels often played the hurdy gurdy because it was easy to carry around with them. Today you can hear it playing traditional folk music.

Pianola Pianola

Imagine a piano that plays itself! This is what the pianola does. It looks like an ordinary upright piano, with a roll of paper set into the wooden casing above the keyboard.

The paper roll has holes punched in it. It turns automatically and the holes act like a code which tells the piano which notes to play.

Some pianolas are worked by bellows, which the pianist pushes with her feet. The bellows blow air, which turns the paper roll. Other pianolas run on electricity.

This drawing is trying to show that the pianola is easy to play – even a baby can press down the pedals.

Gulbransen Trade Mark.

26

Electronic organ

Electronic organ

An organist accompanies gospel singers at the New Orleans Jazz Festival in the USA.

The electronic organ has no pipes. Instead it makes notes from signals produced by electricity. The signals are amplified (made louder) and heard through speakers.

Electronic organs often have two keyboards, called manuals. They also have switches called stops, which the player can press to make an enormous range of sounds. Drums and percussion sounds are built in to accompany the tune the organist is playing.

You can hear the electronic organ played in many rock and pop bands.

Did you know?

In June 2000, music students in Hungary set a record for the largest number of keyboards ever played at once. They played 100 electronic keyboards, programmed to sound like the different instruments of an orchestra.

Keyboards in concert

The piano often accompanies singers and solo instruments in classical music. You can also hear the piano as a solo instrument, for example, in a piece of music called a piano concerto. Here it is accompanied by an orchestra. Many famous classical composers were also brilliant pianists, such as Beethoven, Mozart and Liszt.

Popular dance bands almost always had a piano. During the early 1900s, many people spent evenings out dancing to a band. These bands might also have a clarinet, a double bass and drums to beat out the rhythm.

Lalo Schifrin from Argentina performs at a music festival in France.

Keyboards in concert

The Canadian band Skinny Puppy uses keyboards to make electronic music on a synthesizer.

Pianos play a big part in many jazz bands. Jazz music grew up in America from traditional work songs and spirituals. In jazz, each instrument plays its own tune, and the musicians often improvise (make up the notes as they play them). Jazz music spread through America and the rest of the world during the 1900s. There are many different types of jazz and today you can hear it played everywhere. Famous jazz pianists have included Scott Joplin, Jelly Roll Morton, Duke Ellington and Fats Waller.

Today's rock bands often have an electronic piano or organ, together with electric guitars and drums. Every time you turn on the radio, or listen to a CD you are likely to hear some kind of keyboard.

Words to remember

accompany To play music alongside a singer, or another musician who is playing the tune.

amplifier A machine which makes sounds louder electronically.

band A group of musicians playing together.

bellows Part of an instrument that holds air. You squeeze bellows to pump air through an instrument (such as an organ or accordion) to make it sound.

casing The outer part of a keyboard instrument.

chord A group of notes played together.

classical music Serious music is sometimes called classical music to separate it from popular music. Classical music can also mean music that was written during the late 18th and early 19th centuries and followed certain rules.

composer Someone who writes pieces of music.

concert A performance in front of an audience.

folk music Traditional songs and tunes which are so old that no one remembers who wrote them.

jazz A type of music played by a group of instruments in which each one plays its own tune. Jazz musicians often improvise, or make up, the tunes they play.

keyboard The row of keys on a keyboard instrument.

keys Parts of a keyboard which move a lever to sound a note.

musician Someone who plays an instrument or sings.

orchestra A group of about 90 musicians playing classical music together.

pedal Part of an instrument worked by foot.

pop music Popular music which is entertaining and easy to listen to.

quills The hard middle parts of birds' feathers, used to pluck strings on a harpsichord and virginal.

reed A small, thin piece of metal that vibrates to make a note.

rhythm The beat of the music, which depends on how short or long the notes are.

rock music Pop music with a strong beat, or rhythm.

solo A piece of music played or sung by one performer.

spirituals Religious songs that began among black slaves in the southern United States more than 200 years ago.

stop A lever or knob which changes the sound when pulled.

tone The sound of an instrument.

vibrate To move up and down quickly, or quiver.

Index